FRIENDLY FIRE

THE HOTCHKISS SCHOOL

Author

FRIENDLY FIRE

poems by

Katrina Roberts

LOST HORSE PRESS
Sandpoint | Idaho

ACKNOWLEDGMENTS

Ploughshares: "Blue"

Runes: "Spiritus" (also nominated for a Pushcart Prize, 2005)

The Long Journey: Pacific Northwest Poets: "Skin," "Hunger" (Oregon State University Press, ed. David Biespiel, Fall 2006)

I wish to thank Lia Purpura, Paul Lisicky, Molly Fisk, Chris Merrill and David St. John for ongoing generosity and insights. To Giach Marshall, *grazie.* For inland shelter, thanks as well to Laura Norris, Beth Swanson, Chrisy Jones, and Kirsten Telander. XO to Francie Randolph, kindred spirit in things elemental. And a hug to Karen Babbitt on the coast.

A debt of gratitude to the Whitman College community, the English Department, and especially to George Ball, Timothy Kaufman-Osborn, Pat Keef, and George Bridges.

Endless appreciation to Robin Becker for believing in this book, and to Christine Holbert for making it happen. And a transatlantic wink to Dan Desborough for painting with fire.

Thanks to my parents and Dorothy Roberts Burr—without whom, nothing. And to my husband and children, each day, boundless love—for everything.

Cover art by Dan Desborough.
Author photo by Bunna.
Cover and interior design by Christine Holbert.

FIRST EDITION

Library of Congress Cataloging-in-Publication Data
Roberts, Katrina.
 Friendly fire : poems / by Katrina Roberts.—1st ed.
        p. cm.
 ISBN 978-0-9800289-1-1 (alk. paper)
 I. Title.
 PS3568.O23875F75 2008
 811'.54—dc22

                    2007044331

For Jeremy
For Phineas, Zephyrus & Thalassa

TABLE OF CONTENTS

ONE

TWO

ONE

My love is my weight.

—*Saint Augustine*

BLUE

I stand there under the high limbs of locust
watching my father point a black gun into the air

his arms steepled for the stillness
required to split the proverbial hair

with a BB. I would like to throw a red hat
to catch what will smack from the barrel

but instead the songbird drops fast—a warm
stone through liquid swimming between us.

The stink of yellow sulfur thick. And the twist
of his mouth, like tangled purple boughs

or crossed legs of what he never dreamed he'd hit.
Years after, I will admit only to so much. Blue

moon tomorrow. Do *we* ever get a second
chance? It's what I don't say that speaks loudest.

IMPRINT

Something about a house feels sound: walls and panes
to keep what's in in place; what's out, remote. It's like that

on a boat, too, or can be, though years ago I sailed offshore
all night through gales ravaging waters off Massachusetts'

coast, expecting any moment to feel the wet, black brine
on skin. I saw the sloop splinter in surf, debated what I'd flail

to grasp, counted green lights flashing where there were
none. Rain whipped the rigging ragged, drenched our galley,

pricked the backs of necks where slickers met hats almost.
So when this storm kicks up at 4 AM, wakes my boys with

hail shattering glass the living room's length, I run through
rooms to hold them close; the elder quakes as needles rend

sky, igniting Lynch's field like old flashbulb black & whites.
The cold floods in around us; I cannot say: *we're safe.*

All day a small white hand opening
toward windows—the orchid's second

bloom. Pinpoint of blood intaglioed where
petals meet, the sexual folds, layers of pale

flesh that waft the chastest scent, sweet
breath of a babe in arms—his mother's

milk a spittle-lace of shine dried on flushed
cheeks. February, his third month, no cause

for expiation of any sort, though blossom-talk
calls into question any reason for being as

one is—not gaudy exactly, more blown fully,
teasing, though cloistered on the sill. Beyond

panes, beside lanceted doors of Our Church
of Assumption, two boys aim guns and laugh.

SUICIDE

What the wind carries with it—not promise nor
answer but only the breath of something other.

They'd been boys together, then "lost touch."
How did that happen? Just life stuff I guess,

not much more . . . Rather, what keeps anyone
joined? What with all these different states of

mind, beyond geography. *sigh.* We care most
about ourselves? Because he was angry, he

doused the fallen limbs and struck a match. I
watched it flare and hands click steadily by

the hour of his buddy's service. *Honor,* what
is it? I thought about a mother and a father—

how surely they gazed in wonder at his birth.
All day tears ran with sweat, for what it's worth.

FOOLISH

To think I could live inland, born on the coast . . .
Yet, mostly I'm okay. Sometimes the most

I miss is the reek of salt and the way the picture
keeps changing—the sea's continual fingers

smearing the view. But here: the proverbial
amber waves of wheat, rippling, and whole

swaths of clear sky without interruption do
speak to the longing I secretly harbor to

perch beside water like a gull. They circle
over landfills even this far away, the pull

of briny soups made in ragged tuna tins
with rain, creosote on logs, whiff of shells,

bones, jetsam, flotsam—all smells like home.
Ignis fatuus beneath a phosphorescent moon.

BUFFER

Sky black with ash and soot: who's burning
the fields that ring this town, scorching

stubbled acres of wheat back down to dirt
to recycle nutrients and prepare the earth

for another season? *Don't worry.* They've
disked wide swaths around perimeters, saved

contiguous plots from being licked up
in carving zones no eager flames could hop

though it's true: the plumes of smoke are
frightening. Meanwhile, globe-wide, wars

rage over differences in faith or land to call
home—a stretch of ground, a fence or walls

sometimes all that lies between two peoples
feuding: when breached, each ire's rekindled.

MEAN

My grandmother scolds me for having told a story:
how a balloon wobbling over asphalt toward klieg lights

ringing Home Depot (my son's small hand—two fingers
raised the way Gabriel's often are in Annunciations, gesturing

toward the departing yellow orb, his high voice the wail
of one being torn apart limb by limb), how surely this homing

sun would ride a thermal east above the heartland to find
a beloved great grandmother's window in Pittsburgh, how

she would look out, smiling, and think of him. Not lost,
simply having moved on. She writes: *You're wrong; kids*

need to know the truth. My father told me it was gone when
I let go of mine on the trolley. And the wren, coming upon

shredded rubber strung in high boughs of an elm decades
ago in Red Bank, New Jersey: what did it mean to him?

SUMMONS

I started to conjure what life since I'd be dead
would be for my children: how in spring beds

around the house they might see me poking
through mulch, how they might start out singing

"doe a deer," then find themselves crying for no
apparent reason, how their father would have to

show them which fork to use, how to write notes
of thanks for generous acts, to tie shoes then knot

ties in years to come. Each morning water beat
my skull; I let it run over my limbs, my heart

pounding, dark thoughts compounding: seeds
of something grim waiting to be revealed when

finally I took myself in to a doctor. Beneath
fingers, soap swirled where nodes lay swollen.

MARROW

To will the body's rebound from declivity—
a quick slide when white blood cells hit rock

bottom—is to give oneself over to a lexicon
of dirt, mineral rich and saturated, but nothing

edible. And it may or may not work, host-
cells rejecting the new—rash and nausea

washing over, but hope pokes up and through
in saffron and lilac snouts. Petal soft but

feisty. How they must hold their breaths all
winter to emerge—their deshabille like that

of sparrows bathing in dust. How they kill
her, nearly, to bring her back . . . Meanwhile,

the cats wear mansuetude like new pelts and
cross the kitchen tiles, leaving muddy tracks.

VINEYARD

The vines have gone dormant in December's chill.
Our new son is home from the hospital.

The older boy says *thank you for screaming and throwing
something,* confusing gratitude for apology.

Swallows rise in synchronized spin over the latent rows.
The baby cries all evening; there is no consolation

though always a promise of change for one with dirt
under her nails. Who can cauterize the place where my

boy has left, already turning away when I ask only
that he look at me? His child body, taut like wire strung

between posts. *No, Mama, the baby isn't thirsty.*
Something trellised. Something sweet and bitter at once.

Overhead, scarred moon. I carry our newest into each
room seeking silence. My boy turns in his sleep.

SOMNAMBULIST

Dark kitchen; moon a knife piercing glass
to rinse grey speckled tiles white: I

walk the baby toward sleep—one step,
two, another, listing left and right as though

my mooring line's been cut. It has. What name
exists for this island I visit nightly—lapped

by tongues and tears, hummed lullabies,
whimpers, sighs, the pitch and roll of each

thought, hope, fear a parent could harbor?
How to will the mind's cessation, to fix eyes

instead on a proverbial horizon, let Lynch's
illumined barn be lighthouse steering me

from rocks? Within a stall the mare whose foal
lies at her feet, stands and sways: asleep.

SUNDAY

With our son on his lap, he mows the back field early
before the mercury climbs into three digits. Barely

midsummer and already everything droops by noon.
What will August bring? Blue needles loom—

dragonflies darning dizzy air beneath junipers, hover
to land on shoulders or backs of hands then scribble

off—all day this dance that gets them nowhere other
than where they are . . . Mating? Just hatched? Full

swarm, winging me back to a lakeside hour: I'm five,
my father's thumb spurts blood; in the boat's bilge

the bluing sliced-off tip rolls around until it's fished
from muck. Mom drives through cool pine air to will

a doctor on call: sleepy Sunday; Dad's face, a sheet
of paper. I watched him wilt—as roses do in heat.

ELEMENTAL

Bending glass: unlikely proposition though the propane
glowed blue before me and already, clear rods others

held gave way softly in hands far more steady than mine.
My problem was the torch—combustible, hissing, and

the way this tube resisted; I knew it would shatter, but
pulled ends toward me as the teacher instructed, waiting

for the *crack* that finally came to let it all give way:
invisible, jagged fragments lodged in the soft pad of

palm beneath my thumb—not felt until noticed, then
a throbbing rush of blood swirling the porcelain drain . . .

First, light and space behind my eyes as color seeped
out, then sound, then my legs, gone. How I came to

later in a spray of diamonds—beakers launched by my
body as I fell. Lab over, yet eternal. I'd missed the bell.

DOG

Bernadette's Doberman lunged, his lips
curled back to let white fangs drip

and I ran, despite the leash she tugged.
She tipped her heart-shaped face, smug

with delight, tossed her chin so a ring
of chestnut hair haloed her head, sang

"He's bark not bite," which I know now
all these years later was likely how

her mother, playing bridge behind dark
shades, described her dad, tilting cards

to her mouth so no one could see. *"You
don't believe in God,"* Bernadette cried

after me, who didn't attend St. Mary's
as did all her friends on the block. *Please.*

How can one not love a wick bearing flame, incense
thick about the head, transport of psalm, of song

upheld by every good pilgrim filling pews? What
fine narrative intermediaries choose to believe:

swallowing wine, turning proverbial cheeks to divert
eyes, in fact, from hypocrisy. . . . Am I *en route*

to my own Erebus? Occam's razor would have clocks
chiming wrong hours for no other reason than human

error—no doomsday, no wonder, no ghosts seeping
through rafters to play tricks on this stunned mother.

Beyond glass, a flatbed hovers over fogged vineyards
bearing congeries of twisted metal: old public school

slide, woodstove, mufflers, struts. Inside, a bristly
frenulum links moths' wings for flight, but toward flame.

BURN

A tower of bales suddenly aflame in Yakima makes
news. Not dry enough, a static flash, indeterminate

cause, though vast lost. Next day, crisp grass beneath
the Ford so he clicks it off. But these things, like sparks

from exhaust—we understand them. What of the wick
effect, spontaneous combustion of human flesh: torso

and arms consumed; bare skull, lower legs intact, rooms
left relatively uncharred while the TV-watcher flares,

burns, and burns out? Loneliness is a factor, some
figure; others flat out disregard such stories as fluff.

But sometimes it seems there's only the mind and heart
inflicting cause, body simply providing the ride . . . so

summer long: *being alone, being alone, being alone*
builds until one gives in for something else to start.

DEPRESSION

That he couldn't make for himself even
a can of soup is what I remember; shoulders

rolled over his chest like a hooded bird,
he wept onto the counter. It might have been

January, or earlier, or later. Whatever—I
had "had enough," and said so, stirring red

globs until they dissolved, then spooning
vegetables into a mug. Not that he couldn't

have, but wouldn't. Take care of himself.
A future with children? *He* needed a mother.

God, he was beautiful to look at; and I
believed, truly, in the moment I'd said "yes."

But more than merely cope, I wanted to *live*.
I turned the burner off, then flew the coop.

CANADA

What we don't know *can* harm us. Beside a sedan from California
(two guys chain-smoking the final thirty yards) the baby began

to wail. A moment freighted with such dark cargo . . . not even
out of the country and already tears. Pulled over past the Peace Arch,

all doors swung wide—they stumbled: loose-limbed, raccoon-eyed,
out and away from the car. Not startled exactly; clearly they'd

been expecting the worst all afternoon, waiting to be caught, betting
just when they were flying high into the next free country, everything

would tumble (fat snow, confetti) down. Of course, *they asked for it,
right?* And you, cruising over the border with a quick nod, patting

the baby back into that charmed realm called sleep, smiling through
panes at now-moving traffic and no one in particular. . . . Until one

morning: two spots of blood in a diaper; a veering bus; the sudden
lump in a breast where fingers have always traveled finding none.

MALIGNANT

The term itself crueler than need be, implying *malicious
contrivance* or *vengeful intent* when it's simply another

Tuesday, and a small girl has lost part of her cheek
to a surgeon's knife. *Tabula Rasa.* Yesterday nobody

would have dreamed such a script unfolding: the glacial
wait for pathology, the punch of "I'm sorry" and

everything after. Cloudless day. To pedal the length
of the driveway, she straps on her helmet, her browned

legs pushing to make wheels crunch over gravel—as
though *bravely* for those of us watching (though she

feels no different). Meanwhile, stealthy growth of vines
in beds—how, despite drought, they twine to choke

roses, asters, echinacea—their plucky tendrils lush
and fingering our minds: *what lies in wait for us?*

STAIN

Stained knees and that old word "dungarees":
my father, tongue wedged between teeth

like an unripe plum in his cheek, strides into
view after years. New Jersey yards, Connecticut

lawns, the scrubby patches of grass that clung
to the face of New Hampshire granite, upon

which, like a tentative cat, the house perched.
Summer ending and the man all industry—

readying his plot of earth for sleep, woodstove
stoked and chugging its ash into high, clear

spaces where pointed pine tips reached. A bit
of green, ground into blue threads, and a ring

of syllables filling my head, recalling every
purple fruit. And each with a small hard pit.

A man, an animal, an almond, all find
maximum repose in a shell—so said

Gaston Bachelard. Blame it on the wind.
Blame it on the fog. Eve says, *don't*

change. But how can I not, shot through
as night sky quivering from a star's hurl?

We were just girls together really. I was
wearing it comfortably and it fit. A

neighbor suddenly finds herself allergic
not only to wine but to water—hives

and a closed throat. Llamas scream all
night at the coyotes. You could say I'm

more cauldron than cross. Snakes slink
it off like a diamond-backed argyle sock.

SOMATIC

Because he could see no way out of his body
yet the mass lay broken, he let his mind—

thought's conduit—collapse as tendrils
unwatered too long wither shut to pinch off

leaf or blossom. So that what once flowered
no longer mattered. Some somnolent

afternoon, a Sunday weeks after his funeral,
friends and family gather to lift glasses—

early thaw, spring's cusp—longing to
scissor limber legs through aisles of vines

already budding, to find him amidst neatly
clipped, splayed shoots. *Ahhh, fructiferous*

memory: everywhere they roam, he beams
at them, still so at home in their bodies.

HAPPEN

My baby's at pool's bottom, falling down basement stairs,
lunging for a ball in the path of oncoming cars: nothing

I can do but watch. I startle awake, waiting to hear soft
whimpers of my youngest turning over—heart still

racing, tangled hair matted and sweaty. In giving birth,
look what I set in motion. . . . And what must she have

thought, my great grandmother, humming over rails,
Jersey train crossing the creek at Raritan Bay, early

May 1937, when clear skies beyond windows exploded
with flames of the Hindenburg, nearly home but for

landing? Silk and champagne. A soap bubble defying
odds, steady in arms of unseen gods. Such ingenuity—

praised before floors gave way. Dead when dirt met
them? What happened? She cranes to see, clattering by.

FORGIVENESS

How does water do it? Always smoothing back over
after ruffled landings, explosion of drops its face

wears for mere moments before recomposing itself
when what burns in me *burns in me* . . . longer

than I care to admit. I shelter the grudge, build
a rustic cabin for it in my chest, pound rusty nails

in to anchor a porch where I sit glaring for hours
usually wishing I could simply take a shower

and rejoin my husband for drinks up at the civilized
house. *God, what's with me?* My children's eyes

search my face for signs of what they've done
wrong and I want to hold them, crying: *Nothing,*

you've done nothing but everything right. Often
I can't even remember what kindled our fight.

Summer is leaving, the leaves letting go. Elsewhere
and beyond, the crumbling that comes with war:

a call and response of mortar and flak through which
children walk. Out of the phone: the torn

voice of a woman. *Torn, torn*—as though a yellow
leaf ripped through its veins in falling could

somehow capture terror a mother knows in leaving
her boy and girl in the hands of the stranger

their father's become. It's not forbidden to leave.
But in their making, oaths bind us to trying, ask us

not to break but bend. With each waking or season,
a new skirmish. Elsewhere, bombs dropping. Here,

the raking whisper of a neighbor. Fragile skin of
truth. And rages waged when shades are drawn.

GOD

Black bike tossed in the gully, blown tube and a tire
ridden to its rim. Flat out odd, though theft and flight

make sense. Just one of morning's mysteries. Haul it
out, up the scrub bank, shifting gravel, a steep pitch

like a far off train's wail filling you with panic—
something out of reach yet palpable. Glossy pages

on the kitchen table ringed with spectacles a mug
of coffee makes each time it's placed then replaced:

a magazine litany of babies, dead, from having been
shaken – only 5 to 15 seconds, and their fragile stalks

of necks, and their huge heads, their round eyes bright
with glassy fear, then sometimes blood; limbs gone

slack, crying stopped. Shadows of bars cast across
what's lost in the crib. *My god, where are you now?*

TWO

Love is not consolation, it is light.

—*Simone Weil*

GRAPES

That which you give, you take so freely. Surely
there is a way to see what you are trying to say—perhaps

in rows of bent, brown vines, a few dried grapes
brash magpies didn't find, the rimed lace of puddle-water

that blooms in moonlight each December night, then
melts away. You understand for us the taking isn't easy

yet you leave us standing where we are, rooted in dirt
while our eyes search the sky, waiting. And always

there is budding. But like the boy who rubs his calves—
the throb of growing being pain—we cannot imagine how

light and warmth will find us again. We want to stop
believing in you when you let the child grow to man then

let him veer from a dark road headed home, breath of wine
filling the cab like sin. We want to believe in spring.

AURORA

Shaken awake as children in northern Maine
to see the soundless sky flare red and green

we stood barefooted rubbing bleary eyes
and wondered of the meaning for our short lives

of such a wild display. Would there be another
day? Would we follow scrubby trails with boulders

like the earth's scraped knees around which we'd
find berries enough to fill our pails, again? Seeds

of doubt died as we were led by hand down halls
toward sound and cold milk poured out in tall

clear glasses and warm chocolate chips to fill
our gaping mouths. I know this now: adults still

bow heads together and tip their glasses high
—after children are retucked—and praise the sky.

CLARITY

Tuesday morning at the DMV, not open Monday, so
every plastic seat is taken. TV screen hangs in the corner

above three women talking about a husband. *"Claro que
sí,"* says one, and the youngest, her black mane caught

at her nape with a red clip turns to see which number
has clicked onto the box over the counter. What kind

of devotion brings us all here? *Laws of nature . . .* This
drab building, air charged with ions of anxiety as two

boys stab at keyboards in cubicles nearby. Tapping shoes,
reshuffled news. One man moves across tiles, a grey dove

pecking and poking, impatient with waiting, addressing no
one in particular, so anyone who hears. Organ donor.

Voter registration. The honest revelation of leaning into
goggles to read a string of letters that will not cohere.

CONFESSION

The month I slept in the shadow of the Duomo
on a narrow cot at the Convent of Santa

Caterina, stashing my empties in the armoire
before slipping late into the last pew to hear

Latin incantations, I learned something of
being content alone. Fat patinated doves

shot out a-flap when I swung wood shutters
wide each morning. Married guys hurried

me into toy cars, drove one town over to ply
me with Campari, whose bright gem hue belies

nothing of its bitter bite. Long before night
fell I'd tire of attempted pecks. One's wife,

an officer for *Politzia Centrale,* would arrive
home in an hour . . . I said I'd rather be alive.

VOLITION

Some wear desire like a garment, draped
softly over shoulders, slipping in dimming

afternoon light to reveal pale landscapes
of clavicle and nape that promise years

of shared travel: breezes, palm fronds,
lapping seas. And we could go there, pack

bags with suits for swimming, flip-flops,
hats, bright currency of elsewhere. Once

somebody told me, "Each day is a coin,
flipped, that we can choose or not to spend,

and I am simply unwilling." After that, all
we could do was button our coats, turn

collars against the January night, retrace
our solitary steps through Cambridge streets.

SAVIOR

One thought he could rescue me from myself
the way—with flamethrower, drip torch

and flapper—he'd step from the belly
of a chopper into the very flames eating

through each living thing clinging to rock.
Smoke jumping every summer, he'd walk

a "blackline" over and back, *eye for an
eye, fire with fire;* then, come winter when

rain and ice did it naturally and quicker
he'd head to town, find a board to hammer

and a bed to fill. He'd pick a blue tune, tell
me he wasn't looking for the kind of girl

who skipped church . . . though he'd stay late.
It would've taken me a leap greater than faith.

CLOUDS

Morning's first light streaks their bases pink—luminous
curves, cumulus peach. My baby wants melon

in his hands and mouth, so I slice and slice. By 7:00, flinty
blue edges rose away; nothing warm or gold left but in

minds of those up early. Clouds will thicken, darken; by
afternoon when cold blows in from the west it's no surprise.

Construction across the road, vibrating walls. I consider
concrete foundations, heat milk for a bottle. As children, we

think we can step off from the wing of a plane into chambers
clouds must make in the sky. In his room, shelves of books

about rabbits and trains. We haven't taught our boy anything
of "organized religion." But I take him swimming

at the YMCA, come rain or snow. And faith lets him lie
back—a blonde nimbus—floating in my arms.

LANDING

after the work of Etienne-Jules Marey, 1830-1904

Because he wanted to make visible that
which compels motion, he held

the cat by paws above a cushion, then
let her drop: using dead weight

of her own body to twist around, she
landed on all fours, properly—

defying Newton's mechanical law
re: objects moving. Each of his frames

charts descriptions of things taken
quite often, for granted—walking,

jumping, breathing. And his graphing
devices rendered tracings of a

body's functions, capturing at last
instinct—that which animates invisibly.

FRIGATE

The anesthetist said *sometimes this happens.* It felt
like forever. We leaned in over your body to see what

your face might reveal. What your eyes were seeing
beneath closed lids, we'll never know and you won't tell.

Since we had urged you into surgery we felt responsible.
The ash pallor of skin, how shallow the breath

that curled from your lips and each fine line of sweat
beading high across your cheeks. Once years ago, when

you spoke, we leaned toward the fire. *And they sped over
water in a frigate . . .* we remember you saying, though

what we heard was "forget." Smoke hung in our sweaters
and hair all the next day and for the week after. Finally

you came to to peer at our stricken faces lining the shore
of your bed; splattered our shoes. *I'm back,* you said, *hello.*

DIRECTION

All afternoon, magpies badgering nests in the elm's arms
and a mad flapping of soft grey wings unable to fend off.

New ones—slick, all eye: unseeing, black, fixed on
something else; thin plumes matted flat on skulls, their

bones like interlocking tavern puzzles: impossible, a-
kimbo, now still. And solving the riddle of motion's a trick

only some god knows. Meanwhile, two cats slink, smoke
beneath fat lilacs, seeking what was taken from them

hours ago: a duckling, butter dun down and fierce peep
calling for rescue. Behind the barn, a boy who's almost four

chooses a stick to wave, tucks it beneath his arm, screams
with untethered joy: *I'm shooting you* . . . though he's never

seen a gun. Remember how he clung to your leg as hot air
balloons swelled with fire then rose to fill this morning's sky.

When a boy ducks as his mother lifts her hand for a block
or book on a high shelf, does fear pass through her like a magpie's

shadow across a smooth lawn of green blades, midsummer?
Later, she'll let shower water hotter than she can bear course

over shoulders and head, allow pounding fingers to comb streaming
hair as steam consumes her, thoughts the spinning rings around a small

black hole in tile. She'll think: *No more.* There's no more voice
left in her; from here on out she'll have to whisper. The times she's

yelled stack up within her, hand upon hand like the game kids play.
She's never hit him, though she's held his wrists too tightly. The day

he flailed on the table catching her chin, she could have . . . *Grawk,*
Grawk. They're up there on the wire, black and white: such

clean lines, each wing slashed sapphire, tormenting the old cat
because they can—swift dips and harsh tones—until he runs.

REASON

Because I could is why I did it—lifted the metal disc
to see them scatter and reconvene, how they'd figure

day's bright torch upon their backs, smell of sun
like coins in a mouth or the taste of one's own blood

suddenly blooming on lips. All winter and spring
they'd had to colonize dirt the rich brown of sorrow

only one who's lost something can know. They moved
across each other, discrete seeds roiling in a breeze

though all was still and held, scooting past then circling
back to become black rivulets clotting only to pull

rice grains, their eventual young, down into spaces dark
beneath now roofless tunnels; they moved, no furnishings

but themselves, their puddle spreading beneath a tree's
fixed shadow. Then they sank from sight, releasing me.

What would you call it—this will to grow, to grasp
and suck all that one sees, to sit like a pudgy Buddha

at five months, thumb of his plum-sized hand
wedged between gums while his left rows air madly

so as not to let him capsize, telegraphed drool
spooling into a plush chick-yellow lap? *Oh, dare*

to say! Life: this ocean of pillows, quilts, world
of sweet milk and naps, of numinous light coming to

kiss cheeks, brush lips and knees—shrimp pink
as the sun dives behind old crossed arms of locust.

And why is this hunger lost? Blue eyes blink wide
at the phone, our screeching cats, each sound

giving birth to a laugh that starts in toes, he, now
on his back, has found he can cram into his mouth.

HUNGER

On fishing-line, a nest dangles from a gnarled limb.
In six months' time there will be apples to fill

arms. Where did birds find this filament? Such
active circling and weaving; the dervish love calls

into being. . . . How many eggs hatched? How many
did the cats poach, poised as they are to pounce—

orchard their stalking ground? Wing and fur. This
morning: another gopher, its entrails a smear across

the stoop; yesterday, a good-sized quail, dismantled
like a duster, but wet and plump and warm in a

feline mouth. How ravenous they are, essing our legs
in eights—he, with a hunk gouged from his silver

haunch, snagged on a barbed fence, bits of tape—
worm stuck to the plush beneath his upswept tail.

WHOLE

He clasped his hands so I knew he'd taken the end
off one of his fingers. I saw them stride from the vineyard

with meaning, moving toward me where already I held
open the screen door. It was still attached though

blood in sticky rivulets thick on his wrist had suggested
the worst. He cringed when I doused it out, the sliced flap

opening to reveal more than I want ever to see of his
body; not that I don't love him wholly. I felt anger rise

which is wrong, but fear one harbors for those loved
fiercely makes the mind go weird places. *You must*

take care, I hissed so the baby, spoon aloft, turned
in his chair. Our elder boy danced like a kite on a string

in March weather, wanting to see but unable to look.
I patched him with tape so he could continue his pruning.

LIFT

Because there was no disc, he flipped a rusty metal gate
on its side to smooth furrows the plow dragged. Dirt pulsed;

a gold sweep of late afternoon sun—rich elemental brown
of old blood. Pheasants, flushed like satin bellows, rose over

bleached stalks of thistle toward limbs of high black walnut,
locusts, cottonwoods along banks of Yellowhawk Creek, coursing

hard this March with winter's run-off. When he returned from far
fields, he left his boots at the door beside his son's, simply a tiny

version so that his mind went to the pint-sized violin they'd seen
in a catalogue some months ago. *Bullshit,* he said into the phone as

I came in from town, *you know nothing of my happiness.* I knew
it was his mother. And when he swung to take the milk jug

from my outstretched hand, our boy on my left hip,
I saw a great weight no longer held his shoulders down.

44

VIBRISSA

You don't know I'm here watching you from beyond
the clean new fence, inside glass. What white paint

can hide . . . a multitude of proverbial sins: knots, eyes,
weathered boards. That and spackle—which binds

our lives together sometimes, as well as kids, who grow
daily to resemble one of us more than the other:

your eyes today, tomorrow my nose. So it goes.
Another evening sliding into blackness and you still

at it. *So tired. Won't always be like this* . . . You stare
into cragged limbs of locust, a snow of willows

wafting from the creek, incongruous in May's first
thick heat. Always it's music in movies that tells us

something's imminent or near. But now suddenly
in silence you turn, hand raised, nodding toward me.

BEST

He told us a story of lightning splitting the lone tree
on a hill's top, killing three horses beneath it at once.

They lay that way through winter; come May, their
licked-clean bones gleamed from a bed of green tendrils

and clover. We knew it had meaning, the way he said:
nature takes care to spirit back what's hers; they'd

been his best. We watched him talk, then he stopped.
This comes to me today just as a curtain of white

sweeps the vineyard, buds thrashed by torrents combing
the rows, the clatter on glass waking my napping boy

who stumbles to find me pacing linoleum, leans his
curly head into my leg as animals do, whimpers *when*

will it end? Of course it does, sky lightening first
southwest of here where often we can see what's next.

My students, ones like clear glass vessels radiant
in sun—I could be their mother, but how when I am

still one of them? They pour things out: *how she takes
herself to the clinic; the absent "ex."* I haven't told

about the life I'll bear come fall. Certain things we do
not share. They'll know in time, my belly swelling;

some will be gone by then or wouldn't care. Another
writes of making tea from nettles: *how to touch*

*stinging stalks, how the liquid goes down burning,
how some people flog themselves to feel the needling*

stop. And what's left? Welt, thrumming itch, salt
in a paper cut. It might as well hurt so long as we're

living. Driving past the Exxon, I see the billion stars
a windshield smashed last night makes on asphalt.

GUNS

At one friend's home whole arsenals of guns
litter the lawn—bright plastic shapes my sons

pick their ways between to take proffered
popsicles. Later, on evening news, words

like "ambush," "strike," and "friendly fire"
punctuate glowing clips of wreckage in far

fields where other mothers' children kneel to
aim and pray. And though it's clichéd, truth

be told, I wish one could keep her boys
from growing old and going off to die. Toys

need not rush us there. Instinct? No harm?
An urge to hoist whatever's there, hard-

wired within? Perhaps ignoble, I'm still glad
when one spits on his own: *They're bad.*

Possum, postulant, tell me you're simply playing
dead. You rise to swagger past trashcans, cars, picking your

way on scaly feet (four-fingered, dark, sharp) back out
into the fray. *Come what may.* Waft of the barn cats' kibble

drew you to the stoop where under a bare bulb
flicked on and off, you rattled the plastic dish that called us out

to witness your bumbling (rosary of your tracing), your clumsy
unintended descent: grey football, end to end over the top

step. Your tail a mangy tap-root, a scraped parsnip pocked
with garden dirt, your pointed, pink, wedge-shaped head,

your pale snout gleaming through pewter wire tufts
and pressed to concrete. Blind to our flurry. We have nothing

but the empty dish of our hearts. You don't scare at the door's
click; you circle, sniff, befuddled and unperturbed.

That something can lie so still yet live. There's hope.

HOPE

He comes in the evening when I'm not expecting
company, and I answer his knock half-clad, hair pulled

back in a long tail, face scrubbed pink, bleary
from reading now that the boys are breathing softly

in their corners of the house and light has drained
from the willows. He's looking for my husband but

happy to let me stand with the door propped open, waft
of sweet ale a haze around his head, his dark eyes

glassy, to tell me instead about one land scheme or
another. A dreamer wishing we had money, he wants

nothing but to have reason to hope, and a girl to call
his own would be nice, too. *Did he tell me you were*

going to have another? He gazes at daisies sprigging
cloth across my belly. I nod; his face goes soft.

HOLD

Because we've finished about Paddington, we open
pages onto Misty, though the book begins long

before anyone reaches Chincoteague, with cries
of a stallion bound in the hold of a Spanish galleon,

a greedy captain pacing, eyes on his rigging, debating
which course of action . . . as the vessel falls still

in a lull. *Proverbial calm; charged air.* The hull
splinters moments later—the storm that made velvet

nostrils flare (his 19 mares straining, too, against their
stalls) suddenly realized. My boy rubs his eyes.

Some will survive to nibble tufts of salty sea-grass,
free to roll at last on solid ground. We mark our place

for tomorrow. *Here,* I say, his flat palm against my
belly; when he feels the kick, his eyes grow wide.

LULLABY

Palomino, tiny pope, milky mouselet mine—
we're belly to belly beneath a waxing gibbous moon.

Your necklace of spine fills my cupped left palm
while hummingbird beat of your heart keeps time

at bay, whole moments suspended like felt clouds
held aloft without strings. So what bright architect

conjured this magic, struck the startled woven chords
we hear tonight as you take me blindly between perfect

gums and suck, the sudden rush a gem-faced heaviness
and lightening all at once? Dead stars surely hum

sonatas as you nurse, soft feather of your new breath
on my wrist, small nostrils flaring. And what comes

next is the steady shifting of sleeping beasts, hoof
to hoof, the sacrament of skin, its sweet warm waft.

ZINNIAS

Garish but beloved: magenta, red, peach—each
blossom the size of a small boy's hand outstretched,

please, give me strength. How ragged I grow
in my day long tread of tasks; how I forget to show

my sons a face as open and bright as they deserve
to see. Even cut, you last on your water-skewed

stems within a green glass globe for days, tempting
the world to gaze. *Shake me from my haze; bring*

me to my senses. Besides fatigue, I have no reason
to complain compared to most others our lone sun

shines upon without our even asking. That I can
walk from this table, that each evening a man

turns in the dark asking, "Where are you?"; that I
am able to hold and be held. . . . No matter why.

IRIS

April again, and someone is saying he doesn't care
for the fat bronze irises by the spigot; it's their honey-red

luster this late afternoon—their suede interiors, gloves
turned inside-out—that draws me as cool gusts

rustle coins in the cottonwoods; even those splintered in
last month's storm stand now scribbled the green

of every new thing. Funny how envy shares this hue
meaning to me only purity. How can one not love

these warm petals, an intricate currency of a country
not one's own, dagger leaves and straight stalks hoisting

them aloft to bounce as bees take flight? Today, when
an old friend finally returned from the sealed room

where she wintered over, leukemia spending her body,
her shorn hair gleamed this same copper, and was lovely.

KATRINA ROBERTS, a graduate of Harvard University and the Iowa Writers' Workshop, is a Paul Garrett Fellow and the Mina Schwabacher Associate Professor of English & the Humanities at Whitman College, where she directs the Visiting Writers Reading Series. Her first book of poems *How Late Desire Looks* won the Peregrine Smith Prize. *The Quick,* her second book, was chosen by Linda Bierds for the Pacific Northwest Poetry Series (University of Washington Press), and was a finalist for the Washington State Book Award. Her work has appeared and is forthcoming in journals and anthologies such as *Ploughshares; Northwest Review; New England Review; The Journal; New Orleans Review; Runes; Sonora Review; Best American Poetry; The Pushcart Book of Poetry: The Best Poems from the First 30 Years of the Pushcart Prize; The Bread Loaf Anthology of New American Poets; Never Before: Poems About First Experiences; The Pushcart Prize Anthology XXII; The Long Journey: Pacific Northwest Poets;* and *Short Takes: Brief Encounters with Contemporary Nonfiction.* She and her husband are the proprietors of and winemakers for Tytonidae Cellars in Walla Walla, Washington, where they live with their three small children.